DEREK

The Sheep

LET'S BEE FRIENDS

FOR NiCKY NOO

DEREK THE SHEEP: LET'S BEE FRIENDS

FiRST PubliShed iN GREAT BRITAIN iN 2017 by

BOG EYED BOOKS,
39 COPTEFIELD DRIVE,
BElVEDERE,
KENT, DA17 5RL

1 3 5 7 9 10 8 6 4 2

TEXT and ILLUSTRATIONS © 2016 GARY NORThFiELD

The RIGHT OF GARY NORThFiELD TO be iDENTIFIED aS auThOR and iLLUSTRATOR
OF ThiS WORK haS been aSSERTED by hiM iN aCCORDANCE WITH The
COPYRiGHT, DESiGNS and PATENTS ACT 1988

PRINTED and bound by COMICPRINTINGUK.COM

LOGO deSigned by baxTERandbailey.CO.UK

BRITiSH LiBRARY CaTaLOGUiNG iN PubliCATiON DaTa:
a CaTaLOGUE RECORD FOR ThiS book iS aVaiLabLE FROM The BRITiSH LiBRARY

ISBN 978-0-9955553-3-4

bog-eyed-books.COM

DEREK
THE SHEEP
LET'S BEE FRIENDS

GARY NORTHFIELD

Bog Eyed Books

THE GRASS IS ALWAYS GREENER

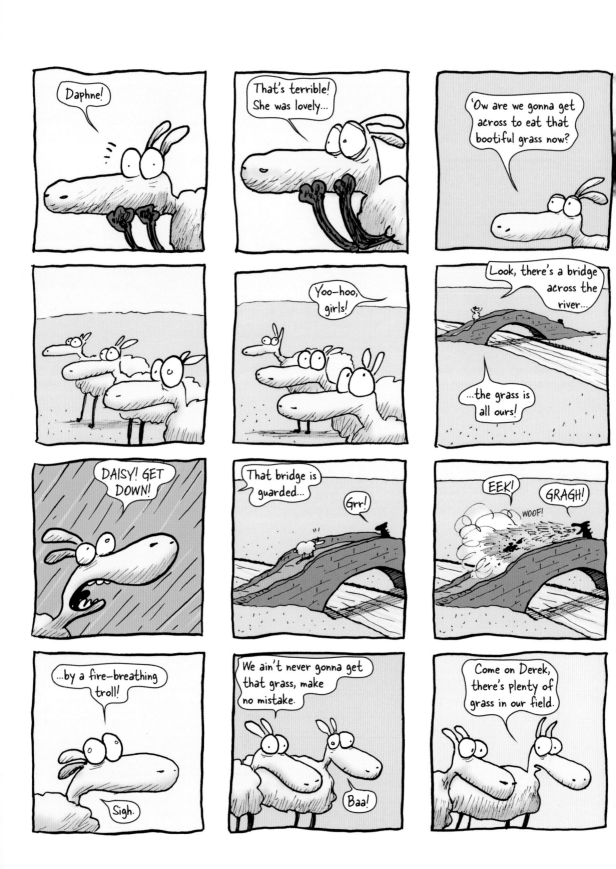

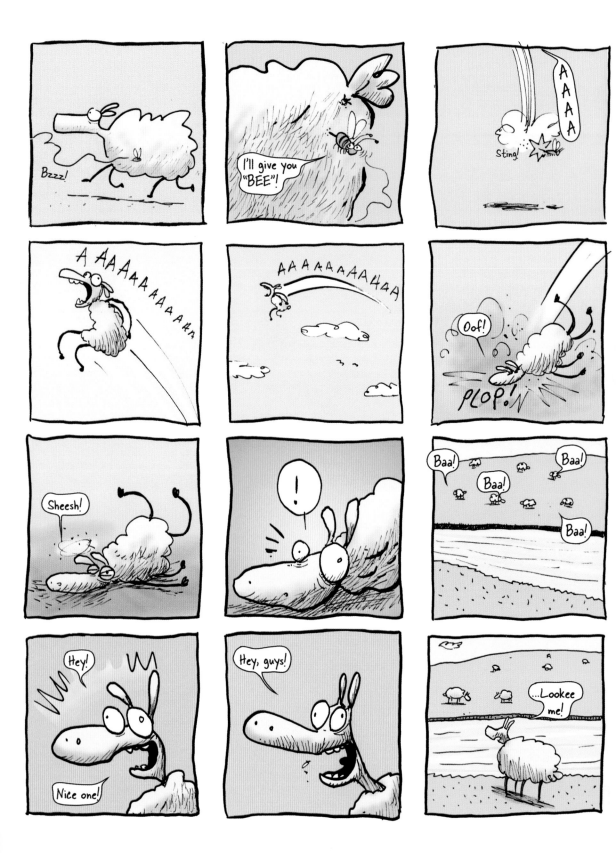

FIELD OF DREAMS

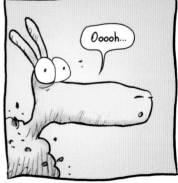

GONE WITH THE WIND

THERE AIN'T NO FLIES ON ME!

IT'S AN ILL WIND

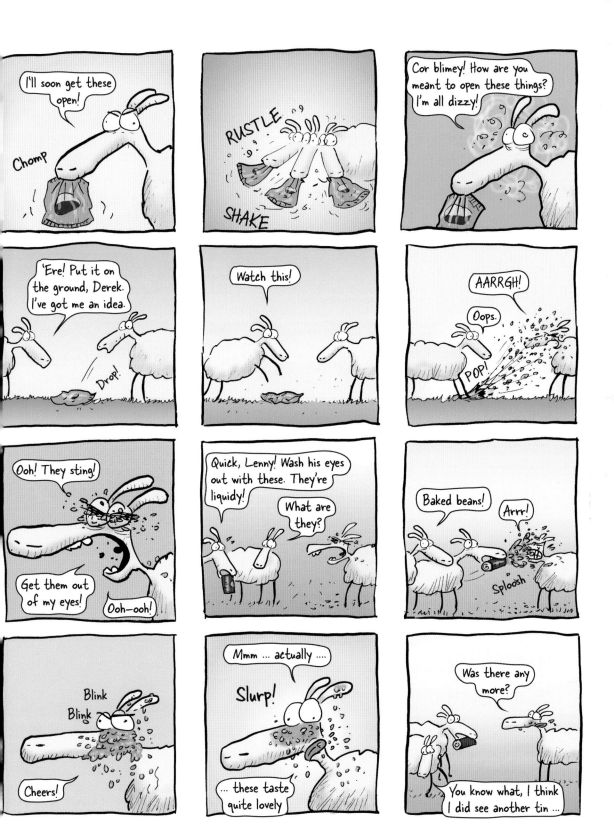

HE'S GOT THE POWER

ONE FOR THE POT

LET'S BEE FRIENDS

NO BUSINESS LIKE SNOW BUSINESS

BAD HAIR DAY

THE BELLS ARE RINGING

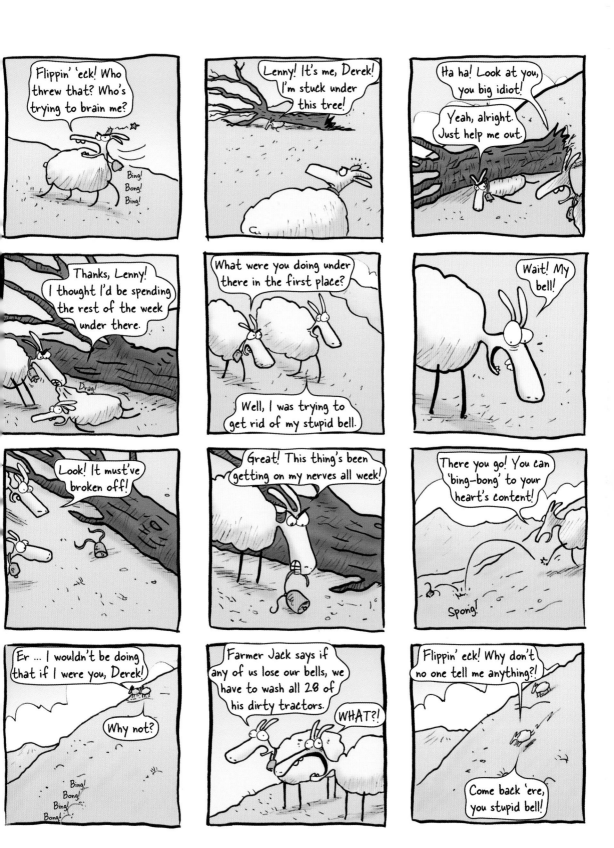

LAME EXCUSE

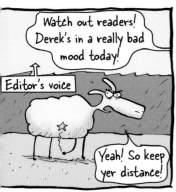

HAVING A BALL

GARY NORTHFIELD has been writing and drawing comics since 2002. He has regularly worked for esteemed magazines such as The Beano, The Phoenix, National Geographic Kids and The Dandy. He has also had books published, including The Terrible Tales of the Teenytinysaurs (Walker 2013), Gary's Garden (David Fickling 2014), Julius Zebra: Rumble with the Romans (Walker 2015), Julius Zebra: Bundle with the Britons (Walker 2016) and Julius Zebra: Entangled with the Egyptians (Walker 2017).